The Child with
Autism **at**
Home

LABOSH
B O O K L E T S

Look for additional Labosh Booklets in
The Child with Autism Series

"Provides parents with the kind of hands-on suggestions that only another parent of an autistic child could have learned through personal experience. A highly recommended resource."

Carolyn T. Bruey, Psy D,
Author of Demystifing Autism: A Guide to Diagnosis
for Parents and Professionals

The Child with Autism at Home

The Home-Life Guide
350 tips for work & play

A part of the Child with Autism series

LABOSH
BOOKLETS

Kathy Labosh
and LaNita Miller

www.laboshpublishing.com

THE CHILD WITH AUTISM AT HOME
by Kathy Labosh and LaNita Miller
Published by Labosh Publishing
A part of the CHILD WITH AUTISM series of booklets
PO Box 588, East Petersburg, PA 17520-0588
www.laboshpublishing.com
email: info@laboshpublishing.com

Disclaimer: Please note that the materials contained in this booklet are based on the author's own experiences and are for informational purposes only. The reader is advised to use his or her own judgement in applying the information to the reader's own situation.

Cover and Interior Book Design by Pneuma Books, LLC
For more info, visit www. pneumabooks.com

Printed in the United States on acid-free paper by UGI

09 08 07 06 05 04   6 5 4 3 2 1

ISBN 0-9744341-2-4
LCCN 2004095598

This booklet and all Labosh Booklets are available in quantity discount for distribution and premium offers. If you are an association, organization, corporation, or individual and you would like to partner with Labosh Publishing to help people with autism and their loved ones, please contact Labosh Publishing at partner@laboshpublishing.com or ask your local autism support group to carry Labosh Booklets. Labosh Booklets are available directly from Labosh Publishing or through your major wholesaler. If you would like to create a custom Labosh Booklet, please contact Labosh Publishing directly. Thank you for your support.

This booklet is dedicated to
Tim Labosh and Bob Miller,
our husbands, whose fidelity,
strength, and understanding
are the foundation of
our happy homes.

Table of Contents

Foreword

Phyllis Kupperman
M.A., CCC-SLP.
Executive Director/Founder
Center for Speech and Language Disorders
Elmhurst / Chicago, Illinois

After giving a day-long presentation in Louisiana last year, I went out to dinner with a group of mothers of children with autism. The conversation around the table was filled with laughter, down-home advice, support, and instant understanding — but mostly laughter. Each knew one another's children and bonded over the struggles the others were going through. What struck me most as I got to know these remarkable women was that they never forgot how to have fun.

Kathy Labosh would have fit right into that group. Her practical advice, her positive philosophy, and her sense of humor shine through. She brings up topics that many parents worry about but hesitate to talk about. She offers ideas without guilt because you know she has walked in your shoes. Her focus is not just on the child with autism, but on the life of the family.

Parents — if you can, find a group of friends

ix

The Child with Autism at Home

to laugh and cry with. But if you are alone out there, take this little book to bed with you, and before you fall asleep, you will find at least one idea that will help you the next day as you live with and love your children with autism. And you will know that you are not alone any more.

Preface

Kathy Labosh

My son Sam's diagnosis of autism caught me unprepared. I looked back on all the missed signs. Cherished memories were revisited in the new light of autism. Future plans were grieved. A desperate search for knowledge ensued. I wanted it to be within my power to cure it. I did not need for my son to be a superstar; I only desired a level of normalcy. Even that modest dream seemed cruelly unreachable.

In the midst of all the despair, I also felt an intense love and devotion toward my son. I searched with hope for every small improvement and marveled at his determination and his joy. He was and is for me a perfect child.

I knew his brother Nicky had autism long before anyone else did. I watched him carefully. He did not respond to his name. The feel of clothes against his skin and the weight of blankets on his small body would make him scream. He never pointed at what he wanted and would cuddle with any woman who vaguely resembled me. I knew inside, but I would have to wait until he was old enough for others to know too.

I thought my experiences with Sam would help with Nicky; they did, but not as much as I had hoped. Although Sam had minimal sensory issues and was verbal, Nicky had many sensory issues and was non-verbal and low functioning. I had to learn new ways of dealing with autism yet again. It seemed like every new issue had to be really thought through. Books on typical childhood development did not address my problems, except to advise seeing a doctor.

I compare my life's journey with autism to a hike up the Appalachian Trail. My ability to complete the journey with joy and satisfaction depends upon my ability to take care of myself physically, to prepare mentally for the hard stretches, to use the right tools to make the trek easier, and to have a good support system in place. But more than anything else, what I have needed is a trail to follow and a map to help me when I got lost.

My booklets are tools that can help you in practical ways on your journey. I have not reached the end of the journey, but I have learned from my time wandering lost in the woods. My desire is to spare you from that. THE CHILD WITH AUTISM AT HOME is a compilation of my best advice on how to keep yourself and your marriage together, how to discipline your children, how to teach them to be a self-sufficient and contributing member of your family. I have even included sections on toys and activities that my children love to help you make your home a happy one.

Some of my tips are unconventional. Families living with autism face many challenges not ordinarily found in typical families. We often change our customary behavior to adapt to the needs of our loved ones. For instance, when Sam and Nicky were young and non-verbal, I could not feed them at the table. Sam would take one bite every couple of minutes while Nicky would gobble his food and anyone else's within reach. In order to keep both boys fed and calm, I needed to feed them separate from each other in their rooms. That was the structure I needed for my family to function.

I let an early intervention class teach my children to eat at a table and then transferred those skills to our home. There will likely be behaviors that your child will learn easier in a school setting. Embrace the help. Often the child is alone in a room with an aide whose job it is to work one-on-one with them. That person gets to leave at the end of the day. Parents of children with autism cannot do that. Do not feel that you are a failure as a parent because others can teach your child things that you cannot.

The Child with Autism at Home

I have asked LaNita Miller, my children's first teacher, and the one who taught them and many other children with autism these skills, to share some of her tips. I would like to claim that I am the super parent who can do it all, but it is better to be someone who realizes her limitations. To survive you have to recognize your need for others.

About the Author, Kathy Labosh

Kathy Labosh graduated from Penn State and worked as an economist. She is now a stay-at-home mom to Sam and Nicky, both of whom are children with autism. It became her mission to help others in similar situations. Kathy formed a Special Education Religion Class and is the author of a specialized curriculum for children with autism. She also received an Honorable Mention for Children's Fiction from Writer's Digest.

About the Author, LaNita Miller

LaNita Miller is the author of beginning textbooks, received her Bachelor's degree in Elementary Education with a minor in Early Childhood Education from Austin Peay State University and her Master's Degree in Special Education from George Peabody College, which is now part of Vanderbilt University. She is currently completing her certification in Behavioral Analysis. She has over twenty years experience in the special education classroom.

The Child with
Autism at
Home

The Attic

Your Mental Attitude

A happy home begins with you. All children are sensitive to their parent's moods, but children with autism are especially so. If they are scared or fearful, they can act out for days or weeks after an event. Some children will even avoid things associated with a traumatic time for life. In order to stay calm, you need to take care of yourself and deal with negative emotions in ways that are positive and build up the family unit.

❶ Make sure you get adequate sleep. A tired person has less control over their emotions and makes poor decisions. If you are not getting enough sleep because your child has sleeping difficulties, please refer to suggestions in the Bedroom chapter.

❷ Decide what is truly necessary for you to do. Do not give up sleep to complete non-essential tasks.

❸ Consider taking a daily vitamin. Our bodies and brains need certain nutrients to work properly. The better supplied they are, the better they do their job.

❹ Eat raw apples to stay awake during the day. They work like a stimulant. Don't ask me why; just try it.

❺ Eat some protein with breakfast—an egg or some milk. I have found that eating only a sugary snack can set me off on a roller coaster of high and low emotions and energy levels during the day.

❻ Get a treadmill. Stress releases hormones into your body that cause the Fight or Flight Syndrome. If you don't want to fight and you can't leave the house because of the kids, a treadmill gives your body a way of releasing the stress in a healthy manner. This also has the side benefit of making you stronger and better able to deal with the kids.

❼ Learn relaxing, stretching exercises like yoga or tai chi. These release the muscle knots in your body where you store tension. This also adds to your physical well being.

❽ Take deep breaths. They cause actual physical changes in your body to relax it.

❾ Limit your expectations of what can get done in a day. The more hurried we are, the more likely we are to lash out.

❶ The Attic

❿ Write to-do lists when the children are asleep. Your mind is more free to wander if you aren't listening for suspicious noises or dealing with the current crisis.

⓫ Break chores down into tiny tasks. For example: gather the clothes, sort the clothes, put the detergent in the washer, and put the clothes in the washer. Our frustration builds when we are constantly interrupted. If you plan for interruptions you won't be as stressed.

⓬ Add to the list during the day, whenever you see anything that needs to be done. It fools your mind into thinking you've actually done something about it, so it will stop nagging you about it.

⓭ Limit how much of the news you watch if it is upsetting to you. You do not need the added stress.

⓮ Read the newspaper. You can pick the news you read and the time when you will read it. Interruptions will not impede your ability to follow the story.

⓯ Get a TiVo or record your favorite shows as you watch them. You can then go back and catch up on what you missed when you are interrupted.

The Child with Autism at Home

❶ Write letters to God. Pour out all the anger, frustration, and negative emotions that you have toward Him and others. Ask for help; ask for forgiveness. Then tear the letter up.

❷ Join autism chat rooms where you can talk to others in similar situations.

❸ Call old friends on the phone to stay connected to your emotional support system. Some of these friendships will taper off, but others will deepen.

❹ Take an interest in your friend's lives. Do not just use them as a place to unload your stress.

❺ Be careful who you call when you are really upset; not everyone understands your situation. Make sure it is someone sympathetic and supportive.

❻ Step outside your house if you need a break but cannot leave. You can still hear everything that is going on in the house.

❼ Take your keys when you go outside. Children playing with the knob can accidentally lock it.

❽ View your children as gifts from God. They teach patience, kindness, and selflessness.

They were given to you because God believes in you.

❷❹ Grieve the future that you wanted, but find joy in the little things. The only place you can find joy is where you are. The only time you can find joy is now.

❷❺ Focus on what your child can do, rather on what he cannot do.

❷❻ Realize it will take repetition for your child to learn anything. You are laying new neural pathways down in his brain. This is only done through repetition.

❷❼ Do not get upset with your child for slow progress. It is not his fault that he has autism and cannot be forced out of it. Expressions of frustration tend to slow down learning, because the child is then afraid to try that activity again. He associates it with getting in trouble.

❷❽ Stop feeling guilty. It is not your fault that your child has autism. It is a worldwide phenomenon. The causes of it are yet unknown. You cannot hold yourself responsible.

❷❾ Realize you are never going to be able to do everything you should. No one can.

The Child with Autism at Home

❸⓿ Find ways to make your child smile. The beauty of their smiles will warm your soul on your saddest days.

❸① Keep your sense of humor. Your attitude can make all the difference in your ability to cope.

❸② Repeat often to your child, "It's a good thing you're cute!"

2
The Master Bedroom

Autism puts the wedding vows of "for better or for worse" to the test. There is a shift of focus from the couple to the child with autism. So much energy is spent trying to help him and make sure that he and the house survive intact. The marriage's needs often take a back seat. There are some small but meaningful things you can do to support your spouse. These tips should be used as suggestions for you and not as a list of demands for your spouse.

❶ Thank your spouse often for the things you've taken for granted. Going to work, watching the kids, and putting food on the table are necessary things for a family's survival. A major cause of marital discontent is the feeling of being unappreciated. You can make your spouse's life much brighter simply by noticing what he or she does for the family.

❷ Tell your spouse what you admire about them. We all have our flaws, but we also

7

have our strengths. When we are feeling down and inadequate, it is good to be reminded of our strengths and how far we've come.

❸ Each spouse should have at least one night of the week that they can count on to be on their own. It is important to have a break from the responsibilities of work and home. It needs to be something they can plan on and look forward to.

❹ Join a group that has nothing to do with autism and everything to do with you. It could be a bowling league, the church choir, a bridge club, a sports team, or an exercise class. It is there that you can have fun and meet people who could become part of the support system for your family.

❺ Have friends over to watch sports or play cards. Let your friends meet your children in their home environment. Allow your friends to get to know you as a couple even if they do not see you together all of the time.

❻ Check to see if the local Office of Mental Retardation has Family Driven Funds which can be used by your family for respite care. They usually supply a list of respite care providers.

❼ Enjoy your break.

❷ The Master Bedroom

❽ Arrange to have regular time away from the kids as a couple. You are a different person when you are relieved of the responsibility for the children. You need to see that underneath it all the marriage is still intact.

❾ Everyone responds to having a child with autism in an individualized way. Try to understand and respect your differences.

❿ Realize that your child's autism may have a genetic component. One or both of you may be mildly autistic. That person's ability to cope with certain stresses might be impaired. You need to be patient with yourself and your spouse.

⓫ State the obvious. It is not obvious to everyone.

⓬ Be patient with repetition. People do not always remember who they told what. It is better to be told a thing a couple of times, rather than not to be told at all.

⓭ Deal with unresolved pain. Avoiding a topic deepens the pain and prolongs the healing process.

⓮ Understand that your spouse is not superman or superwoman. Your emotional needs are not going to be fully met by your spouse. They do love you; one person just cannot meet all the demands that are placed on them.

⓯ Redefine love in terms of commitment rather than romantic ideals. The children will probably eat the candles and destroy the flowers. Love is about doing what it takes to keep the family on solid ground and caring about what happens to the other person.

⓰ Watch your assumptions and question them. Many arguments have been started because someone did not understand what was really going on and filled in the blanks.

⓱ Apologize. It is the quickest way to end an argument and get an apology in return. People will listen to you better if they know that they have been heard and that you care that they were hurt.

⓲ Find something you can both agree on and build from there.

⓳ Ask for help in a positive manner. Say, "Could you open the door for me, please?" instead of, "Can't you see I need help with the door?" The first approach affirms your spouse; the second way tears them down. Your spouse cannot read your mind. Their thoughts are on their own problems. Respect that.

⓴ Say, "Did you get a chance to..." rather

than "Did you..." This reflects your knowledge that your spouse has many responsibilities and pressures.

❷❶ Stress and sex are physically incompatible. If you are going to have sex, you both need to relax first. A back rub, a hot shower, or non-sexual physical affection need to come first. If your spouse is stressed, he or she will not be able to perform sexually.

❷❷ Find ways of making physical contact with your spouse during the day. A hug, a kiss, or a hand on the shoulder will bind you together and reassure them that you are in this together.

❷❸ Avoid things that will unnecessarily add stress to your family life. Adultery, drugs, or alcohol abuse can easily founder a marriage.

❷❹ Beware of well-meaning but toxic friends. They sympathize in a way that encourages resentment toward your spouse. Find a friend who understands that a broken marriage is a lifetime of pain for all involved—especially for the kids.

❷❺ Do not mention your friends during an argument. Your spouse really doesn't want or need to know what so-and-so thinks of them. That person only has a one-sided biased view

The Child with Autism at Home

of the problem. Your spouse will probably end up forgiving you, but they'll probably never feel comfortable around your friend again.

❷ Take the belief that no matter how inadequate the results, both of you are really doing your best. Forgive the shortcomings, because they truly are on both sides.

3
The Bedroom

In order for you to get adequate sleep, your child needs to get adequate sleep. Most sleeping problems are actually sensory issues. Your child may be cold, hungry, or hyperactive. The bed cover or pajamas could be uncomfortable, or he may be experiencing a floating feeling when he lies down. It is a matter of trial and error to discover the problem.

❶ Use pajamas with the tags removed.

❷ Wash bed sheets and clothing with detergent that is free from perfumes, dyes, bleach, and bleach alternatives.

❸ Use pajamas that are plain. Appliqués, raised lettering, or pictures can feel uncomfortable.

❹ Use pajamas that have feet and a zipper if your child tends to kick his blankets off during the night.

❺ Get a larger size, cut off the feet, and put

13

the pajamas on backwards with the zipper down the back if your child knows how to undo the zipper.

❻ Cut off the arms and legs of the pajamas to use during the summertime.

❼ Raise the temperature of the house at night if your child will not tolerate blankets or the pajamas.

❽ Relax an upset child by firmly stroking his legs and feet. It gives him sensory input to focus on.

❾ Cover him with blankets after he is asleep.

❿ Get plain sheets. They can be afraid of the animals on their sheets.

⓫ Switch to flannel sheets. They are softer and warmer in the wintertime. Kids will sometimes accept them even if they don't like regular sheets.

⓬ Place pillows on the floor along the edge of the bed. If the child falls out of bed, he will land on the pillows. Sometimes they don't even wake up.

⓭ Install a ceiling fan with lights. Use the fan during the summer to keep the child cool and the lights are hard for your child to break.

❶❹ Watching a ceiling fan can be relaxing for some children.

❶❺ Have them sleep in a mini pup tent if they like small, enclosed spaces.

❶❻ Use a very firm mattress if your child likes to sleep on the floor. He is probably getting a floating feeling. He is not getting enough sensory input from his body to know where he is.

❶❼ Tuck him in very tightly. It helps him feel secure and that he is not going to fall out of bed. It also increases the sensory input to his brain.

❶❽ Put a TV connected only to a VCR/DVD player in the child's bedroom. The TV should be at your child's eye level when he is going to sleep. Place the TV on the floor if he is on the floor or at bed height or a little higher if he is sleeping on a bed.

❶❾ Turn on the TV and place your child in bed. Sometimes the only time a hyperactive child stops is to watch TV. When they get tired or overtired they get very upset and more active. If you can stop them to watch TV, it gives their body a chance to go to sleep. (This is not recommended for typical children.)

⑳ Play a video that they enjoy but have seen many times before. They will be able to close their eyes and follow along.

㉑ Put the volume very low. They will have to be quiet to hear the video.

㉒ Do not turn off the TV. It will go to static after the video is over, because it is not connected to anything but the VCR. This will also provide a white noise that will block other sounds from waking them up.

㉓ Wake them up in the morning the same way. Turn on their favorite video and turn the volume up. It will wake them up slowly and in a good mood.

㉔ Use low music if a video is too stimulating.

㉕ Do not let your child nap for long periods during the day. It increases the chances that they will wake up in the middle of the night ready to play.

㉖ Let your child stay up until they are sleepy, and then put your child to bed. It helps associate the bed with sleep in their minds. If you put them to bed before they are sleepy, they will want to play, and a battle will ensue. Then they won't want to go to bed at all, because they will associate it with a fight.

㉗ Do not let them sleep anywhere but in the bedroom, preferably on the bed.

㉘ Gradually move the time your child goes to bed earlier in the evening. Start with ten minutes earlier.

㉙ Read to your child if he enjoys books. The goal is to keep the child still in bed long enough to fall asleep. If the book is one he knows very well, he can follow it with his eyes closed.

㉚ Move him out of your bed into his bed if he has been sleeping there. Lie down beside him on his bed. Let him hold your hand or hair, so he feels secure.

㉛ Sit beside the bed on the floor. Let them snuggle with your arm or touch you.

㉜ Sit beside the bed just out of reach. Stay with them until they fall asleep.

㉝ Turn out the light if the child continues to get out of bed. Most children with autism do not like the dark. The lights can go back on if he gets back into bed.

㉞ Do not leave the lights on overnight. It is

not good for the child's eyes. Leave a light on out in the hall, or let the light from the TV provide minimal light.

❸❺ Get melatonin made into a flavored troche at a compounding pharmacy. This will help your child feel sleepy. It is not a sleeping pill. The body naturally produces melatonin when preparing to sleep. Your child may not be producing enough.

❸❻ Ask your pediatrician for a prescription medicine if nothing will get him to sleep.

❸❼ Warn your child five to ten minutes before you begin the bedroom routine. It gives them time to stop what they are doing and men-tally prepare for the transition. This is also useful for bath time and other transitions.

The Corner

4

Children with autism have a reputation for having disciplinary problems. Often they do not understand what you want, or you do not understand what they want. Requests need to be phrased properly and be within their skill level. People often underestimate how long it takes for a child with autism to process a verbal request and how long it takes the child with autism to learn a task. The children need a clear, consistent manner in being disciplined.

❶ Start with the assumption that your child did not understand what you requested. Make your response a teaching experience rather than a punishment.

❷ Pause after making your request. Give the child at least a minute, maybe more, to process what you said.

❸ Let them show you what they want by offering your hand and letting them take you where they want to go.

The Child with Autism at Home

❹ Release their hand if they are trying to get away from you. See what it is they want. My son once fought so hard to get out of my one hand, only to go to the other one. My rings were hurting his hand.

❺ After you have let them communicate what they want say either yes or no. They will accept your answer better, if they know they have been heard.

❻ Let your nos, sound like, "NO!" This is said in a firm voice, but not by shouting which, can add to your child's anxiety. Children with autism have a hard time discerning emotions. They need clear signals.

❼ Let your no mean no. Children with autism can be extremely persistent. If they continue to disobey, they need to be removed from the situation, or the prohibited object needs to be removed. It is expecting too much to have your child exercise self-control when the object is continually in view and within reach.

❽ Think before you say no, if you know you are probably going to change your mind.

❾ Reframe your answer if you want to change your mind. For example, "No, we cannot go to the pool now, but we can go at six o'clock."

● The Corner

❿ Let your yes mean yes. If you said you are going to the pool at six o'clock, go.

⓫ Make them apologize to everyone involved with their inappropriate conduct. For example, if your son spat at another child at camp. He will apologize to the camp counselor, the camp nurse, the child's aide, and the child. Learning how to say, I'm sorry is an important social skill.

⓬ Make them give restitution to the injured party. For example, if your child's favorite snack is Skittles, he will give Skittles to the child he spat.

⓭ Have them correct their mistakes. If they took all the flatware out of your drawers, have them replace it. You will probably have to physically show them how to do this by placing your hand over their hand and by doing it together.

⓮ Have them clean up their own messes. If your child spills juice on the floor, have him get a paper towel and clean it up.

⓯ Be cross when pointing out a serious error, but be effusive with praise when they are correcting it.

⓰ Place broken objects in front of their face

when you are talking to them. They need a visual clue as to what they did wrong.

⓱ Do nothing if the child throws a temper tantrum in public. Wait until they get it out of their system and then continue with what you were going to do.

⓲ Make a business card that says: "My child has autism. I'm doing the best I can. If you want more information regarding autism, please contact the Autism Society of America at 1-800-3AUTISM." Pass the card to curious onlookers and continue to focus on your child.

⓳ Learn the difference between a temper tantrum and a panic attack. Remove a panicked child from the stressor. It is extremely important that your child trusts you to protect him from perceived threats. You need to slowly desensitize him to feared objects.

⓴ Send your child to his room if he throws a temper tantrum at home. He can throw as a big a tantrum as he wants but you do not have to see it or hear it.

㉑ Reverse the locks on your child's door so that the locking mechanism is on the outside. This prevents the child from locking himself inside the room.

22

❷❷ Time out minutes should correspond to the age of the child, usually lasting one minute per year of age. Let them have a timer so they know when they are done.

❷❸ If the child will not stay for a time-out, lock him in his room for the appropriate amount of time. This is where the timer comes in handy. You will let the child out when the timer goes off, regardless of how they are behaving. If they act up are still acting up or again, you can put them back in their room, but a non-verbal child will not understand if you keep increasing his time out because he is acting out. He will have a better chance of understanding if he keeps getting sent in and not released until the timer sounds.

❷❹ Apply the ten-second rule as an alternative. After the time out is finished, they have to be quiet for ten seconds before they can get out of their room. Start counting to ten out loud. Every time they act out, start over at one.

❷❺ Count down the number of times a child can do something if he is stuck in a repetitive action. Say, "OK, three more times, two more times, one more time. That's it. Come give me hug. Now go find something else to do." This prepares them mentally for stopping. It is also a skill, they can use for themselves later on in life.

The Child with Autism at Home

❷❻ Make the countdown a positive experience. A negative experience will add to the stress and the need to do something compulsively.

❷❼ Give a child who bites himself a teething toy to replace his arm. See if you can fix the cause of his frustration.

❷❽ Remove objects of obsession from sight if they are inappropriate or affecting their quality of life. You cannot discipline an obsession away. You may be able to return the object at a later date but do not be too hasty.

❷❾ Write out rules for a child who can read, or use pictures if he cannot. Children with autism are visual learners, and they will remember a written note but not spoken directions.

❸❶ Tell them often what a good child they are. Children with autism live for praise, and they can be very easily crushed. They will live up or down to the way you see them.

❸❶ Find things they are doing right and praise them. Children need to know that it is possible to please you. They will repeat the things that give them a reward. If you heighten your attention, you'll likely find that your child is actually GOOD most of the time. If you are always angry at them, their reward might be getting back at you.

❸❷ Make sure your child has adequate food and sleep. Tired and hungry children act out.

❸❸ Figure out WHY your child is doing a particular behavior. He may be able to get the same result in a more appropriate way.

❸❹ Calm yourself if your child is upset. Your child will never be calmer than you. They often mirror your emotions.

❸❺ Hug and kiss your children often. Happy children do not act out as much as unhappy children.

LABOSH

5

The Family Room

There are a number of fun activities and art projects that you can do with your child. These play activities stimulate their senses and provide interactive play with family members.

❶ Run scarves through your child's hands and around his neck. It tickles and has a silky feel.

❷ Flap with the scarves. They like to see the colors and the fabric move.

❸ Cover the table with protective paper and let the child do finger painting. Let them make hand prints or just rub it over the paper.

❹ Paint with shaving cream on black paper. It has a nice smell and texture to it.

❺ Bury small prizes in a box of dried beans. Let your child dig through the beans to find the prize.

● The Family Room

● Seal the box with beans, and use it as a noisemaker they can shake.

● Hide trinkets inside a ball of non-toxic modeling clay, and have your child manipulate the clay until he finds the object.

● Fill a dishpan with warm water and dishwashing bubbles. Place it on your deck, patio or balcony. Let them splash and wash various waterproof toys. They have fun and the toys get clean.

● Give them sponges to fill with water and then squeeze dry.

● Let your fingers walk up your child's body from his toes to the top of his head.

● Blow on his belly.

● Walk slowly toward your child with your fingers wiggling in front ready to tickle him. Chase him around the house until you catch him and tickle him.

● Tickle him just under his ears, under his chin, under his arms, on his belly, behind his knees, and on the bottom of his feet.

● Tickle them with feathers or feather dusters.

The Child with Autism at Home

❶❺ Make an art project with glitter and glue. They love shiny glitter.

❶❻ Shake pom-poms over their head or on their belly. Let them play with pom-poms. They make an interesting sound and tickle.

❶❼ Have them run and jump on bubble wrap. Everyone loves to pop those bubbles.

❶❽ Roll and bounce your child on a large exercise ball.

❶❾ Teach them to put their hands out to stop their forward momentum on the ball. Children with autism often do not have that skill and will bang their heads. This is a very useful skill to have if they trip.

❷⓿ Wrap them in a blanket and have two people swing them.

❷❶ Cover them with a blanket and tickle them through the blanket.

❷❷ Give strong hugs. Deep pressure feels very good to them.

❷❸ Imitate their happy noise. Try to start a conversation with your child using his happy noise.

6
The Playroom

Everyone wants to know what presents to give to children with autism for their birthdays and holidays. Toys with high sensory input that require little or no manual dexterity are good. Children with autism can have a passion for numbers and letters. Others have a particular object that fascinates them. Know your child's passion and work with it. The following is a list of toys most children with autism will like.

❶ Magnadoodles – it is easier for your child to draw with a magnetic pen than with a pencil or crayon.

❷ Mini-trampoline – they love to bounce. Supervise the jumping so they do not fall on something that could hurt them.

❸ Sit 'n' Spin for children who like to twirl.

❹ Nerf balls for children who throw things.

❺ Vibrating ball – they love the way it shakes.

The Child with Autism at Home

❻ Spinning toys.

❼ Windup toys.

❽ Toy cars.

❾ Koosh balls and animals.

❿ Play Doh — it has a good texture and is easy to manipulate. Make sure it is non-toxic.

⓫ Crayons — make sure they are non-toxic as they are often eaten.

⓬ Silly putty.

⓭ Books that make sounds.

⓮ Calculators — for children who love numbers.

⓯ Easy readers — for children who are learning to speak.

⓰ Videos and DVDs.

⓱ Flashlights.

⓲ Viewmasters.

⓳ Kaleidoscopes.

⓴ Snow Globes.

❷❶ Slinky – it will not last long, but your child will love it.

❷❷ Stress balls – balls that you can squeeze or mold.

❷❸ Squeaky toys.

❷❹ Beanie Babies.

❷❺ Floppy stuffed animals.

❷❻ Gumby or other one-piece dolls – action figures are quickly dismembered.

❷❼ Tickle-me-Elmo.

❷❽ Talking Dora the Explorer.

❷❾ Teletubbies or other favorite cartoon characters.

❸⓿ Tracking beads – they like to push the beads on the convoluted wire tracks.

❸❶ Large Legos.

❸❷ Simple wooden inset puzzles.

❸❸ Glitter wands.

LABOSH

7
The Music Room

Some children are quite gifted with musical instruments; other children just like to bang on anything that makes noise. Music is a good way of introducing information into their minds. Many children will recall words that were sung to them.

❶ Piano – let your child play on the keys. Try lessons if they show an avid interest. The Suzuki method teaches them to play by ear. The traditional methods teach them to read notes. Determine which method is best for your child.

❷ Maracas —they are easy to handle and make noise while a child is bouncing.

❸ Tambourine – can be used with one or two hands. Teach the child to bang the tambourine against his other hand.

❹ Rhythm sticks – similar to the clapping motion.

❺ Electronic keyboards – SEE PIANO.

❻ Bells – are simple to use.

❼ Rainsticks – mimic the sound of rain when they are moved.

❽ Karaoke – some children love to hear their sounds through a microphone.

❾ Make up silly songs about things you want to teach them.

8
The Kitchen

The kitchen is probably the most angst-filled room in the home. Children with autism are frequently very picky eaters, and researchers are always coming up with new things for you to stop feeding your child. Children with autism sometimes do have digestive problems. Some children are helped by a gluten-free and casein (dairy) free diet. Please check the labels or go to www.gfcfdiet.com for up-to-date advice. Please note: This is not medical advice and you should consult with your physician regarding dietary questions and other medical issues.

❶ Do the giggles test to determine if your child might do well on the gluten-free , casein-free diet. Feed your child any grain and cheese mixture – pizza, macaroni and cheese, or a grilled cheese sandwich. If he gets the giggles shortly thereafter, he might not be digesting the food properly.

❷ Check for diarrhea the next day. If your child is not digesting gluten or dairy properly, it can come out in the form of diarrhea or constipation.

❸ Try this diet if your child tantrums on a regular basis.

❹ Give the diet a try for three months and see if you see any noticeable changes.

❺ Gluten-free and dairy-free foods can be found in health food stores and off the internet.

❻ Snacks children with autism often enjoy are: Cheese-flavored crackers, cheese curls, Swedish fish, gummy bears, smarties, raisins, chewing gum, pretzels, Mike and Ike candy, Jell-O, and Mini M&Ms. (Some of these snacks do include gluten or casein.)

❼ Use the one-bite method to introduce new foods. If they take one bite, they can have a piece of their favorite snack. Alternate bites until the plate is empty.

❽ If your child enjoys salty snacks, try foods like ham or bacon with a high salt content first. (Not for those on a kosher diet.)

❾ Give raw carrots to a child when their molars are coming in. They like to bite down hard on things during this process.

The Child with Autism at Home

❿ Introduce ketchup. If the child enjoys eating it, try adding it to new foods that you are introducing.

⓫ Introduce your child to popsicles. You can use them as an ice pack for the mouth or to rehydrate a child who cannot keep anything down.

⓬ Try using plastic utensils if your child will not eat with metal utensils. Some children with touch sensitivities have problems with the metal ones.

⓭ Ask an occupational therapist for adapted utensils.

⓮ Dip the utensil in your child's favorite juice. This will give them practice accepting the utensil before introducing food.

⓯ Dip the utensil in peanut butter or yogurt (not for those on a dairy free diet). These foods will coat the utensil increasing the odds of successful eating.

⓰ Give non-preferred foods before family time when you can devote your full attention to feeding your child.

⓱ Make sure your child is hungry before offering non-preferred foods.

⑱ Give preferred foods during family meal time. This will keep the family meal time enjoyable.

⑲ Use a cushion disk or doughnut to help them stay in their seats.

⑳ Use a booster chair with arms or an adult chair with arms. Push the chair in so the arms are under the table.

㉑ Use a timer to show your child how long you want them to sit. Work up the time gradually. Be realistic regarding how long you expect a young child to sit.

㉒ Reward success with a favorite activity when the timer goes off.

㉓ Give attention to appropriate behavior; ignore inappropriate behavior.

㉔ Save preferred activities for time at the table after the food is eaten.

㉕ Use fold-top sandwich bags that can be opened easily in packed lunches.

㉖ Slightly tear each package to make it easier for them to open it.

㉗ Unscrew each bottle lid and then retighten

it. This allows them to open the bottle easily without making a mess.

9 The Study

Both the high-functioning and low-functioning child need help to build vocabulary and learn concepts. The high-functioning child who is mainstreamed often has trouble studying for tests, because the material is geared for the typical learner. Tips 1–14 will help you prepare your mainstreamed student for tests in the classroom. These tips can be adapted for the lower-functioning child. Tips 15–23 are for the lower-functioning child.

❶ Ask to have a list of the important facts and definitions that he will need to know for the test.

❷ Write the facts on two index cards. Write half of the fact on the first card and the other half on the second card.

❸ Write the definitions on two index cards. Write the word on first card and the definition on the second card.

❹ Work on only two or three new card sets

a night. You can increase the number of new facts if the child learns quickly, but it is best to start slowly.

❺ Have your child read the facts and definitions three times from the cards.

❻ Place the cards on the table, words on one side of the table and definitions on the other side. Have your child match the word card to the definition card. Increase the number of cards on the table as new cards are introduced for repetitive review.

❼ Do not exceed five card sets on the table. Rotate the card sets until all the cards have been used at least once. This will keep it from being overwhelming as well as reinforcing what he has already learned.

❽ Reward correct responses.

❾ Prepare for a multiple choice test by placing on the table one definition and four word cards. Have him pick the correct one.

❿ Prepare for a true or false test by matching the words with either their correct or incorrect definition. Have them tell you whether it is true or false. Do this only after they have all the definitions mastered. Doing it too early could confuse them.

❾ **The Study**

⓫ Prepare for a fill in the blank test by only placing the definition card down and have your child say or write the correct response.

⓬ Prepare for an essay test by placing the word card down and have him write the definition.

⓭ Prepare for a labeling test by placing an unlabeled map or diagram on the table. Make little labels. Work on correctly placing two new labels a night until the child can do them all.

⓮ For deeper understanding of the underlying academics, check Labosh Publishing textbooks designed for the autistic learner. They use pictures and hands-on activities while building language skills.

⓯ Use photographic flashcards to build language for younger students.

⓰ Buy a book on the basics of Applied Behavior Analysis. See resource list at the back of this booklet.

⓱ Label objects around the house if your child is a reader.

⓲ Act out verbs. Make it a game where your child gets to order you to jump or clap.

The Child with Autism at Home

❶❾ Place your hand over his hand to help your child do what you want. Say the action word while you do it.

❷⓿ Place their hands on an object and tell them its name.

❷❶ Take photos of the people that they see frequently. Review the cards before meeting those people.

❷❷ Take photos of the places they go on a regular basis and turn them into flashcards.

❷❸ Place the photos on a board or strip to make a picture itinerary of the places you are going and the people they will meet. Children with autism do better if they can prepare themselves for what is about to happen.

10
The Bathroom

Your battles over personal hygiene are likely obvious. Ask for help from the school if you need it. They can tell if you are having problems brushing your child's teeth or getting him to take a bath. It is hard to admit failings in these areas, but please do ask for help if you need it.

❶ Have your child play with warm, soapy water in a bucket or small tub outside if he does not like the bathtub. Give him toys to splash with, and make the experience an enjoyable one.

❷ Let your child play with warm, soapy water in the sink. Put soap bubbles on his head as a game. Let him see himself in the mirror with bubbles on his head. Put some on your own head.

❸ Spread a damp face cloth over your spread-out hand to create Face Monster! Playfully chase your child around the house calling out, "Face Monster." Have the Face Monster swallow your child's face.

❹ Draw a bathtub with warm soapy water. Put in his favorite toys. Just let him play.

❺ Take a damp face cloth and create Bath Monster and wash his tickle spots, under his chin, behind his ears, under his armpits, and his belly button.

❻ Use the damp face cloth to wet his hair. Make this part of the Bath Monster routine.

❼ Put a small amount of shampoo between your hands. Lather it up with a small amount of water. Start placing the lather on his head.

❽ Have the child lie down in the tub. Gently lap the water up to rinse off.

❾ Have the child lean partly back and use the bucket to rinse it off.

❿ Get a hose attachment for the shower head and carefully direct the spray.

⓫ Use a cloth over their eyes if you have no choice but to use a straight dunk of the bucket.

⓬ Check out the dry shampoos often used in

nursing homes for patients that cannot be bathed.

⑬ Wipe your child's teeth with a wet, terry cloth face cloth if they will not let you brush their teeth. The rough texture will help clean the teeth and protect your fingers if he bites.

⑭ Give them a clean, wet toothbrush to put in their mouth.

⑮ Try an electric toothbrush. Your child may enjoy the sensory stimulation.

⑯ Use non-fluoride toddler toothpaste until they learn how to spit.

⑰ Have spitting contests in the sink. This is one skill they enjoy learning.

⑱ Relax about toilet training. It is going to be a long time before your child learns, but most eventually do learn.

⑲ Diapers are available through Medical Assistance with a prescription for incontinence.

⑳ Watch to see if your child soils his diaper at certain times of the day.

㉑ See if he has a favorite spot he visits when he needs to go. That is a sign that he is aware that something is coming.

The Child with Autism at Home

㉒ Give your child water to drink if he is constipated. Water quickly stimulates the digestive system to help the body push.

㉓ Get behind your child if he has smeared feces on himself. Put two fingers under each armpit. They are usually the cleanest spots and you can control his arms as you guide him to the bathtub.

㉔ Soak your child in the tub to coax off any dried feces if he has had a soiled diaper on for a while. It is gentler on the tender skin than wiping firmly.

㉕ Teach potty training skills in small chunks—pulling down his pants, sitting on the potty for a few seconds. Build the skills slowly. Reward each small step.

㉖ Show your child potty videos and read the potty books.

㉗ Have the same gender parent or sibling model appropriate toileting.

㉘ Write out the steps if your child can read, or make a picture schedule for a child who cannot read.

㉙ Use looser diapers on a child who finds the pressure from a diaper comforting.

㉚ Read TOILET TRAINING INDIVIDUALS WITH AUTISM AND RELATED DEVELOPMENTAL DISORDERS by Maria Wheeler.

㉛ Switch to cloth underwear when your child can use the toilet but lacks the incentive. The feeling of soiled, wet clothing is unpleasant. See the Broom Closet chapter for cleaning tips.

The Broom Closet

11

When you have a child with autism, you develop a detachment to material possessions that would be the envy of a medieval monk. You look upon all objects with an eye for what your child could do тo it. Sigh and move on. This section is tips for keeping your remaining possessions clean and in working order.

❶ Use a carpet cleaner designed for pets when cleaning urine or fecal matter from your carpet.

❷ Soak the remaining stain with water and press a disposable diaper into the wet area. The diaper pulls the dirty water up and removes any remaining residue.

❸ Use a diaper wipe to clean surfaces if you have run out of cleaner.

❹ Check door jambs, door knobs, and light switches for possible fecal matter as well as the walls at the child's arm level. Check furniture he may have sat on.

❺ Spray mattresses with the pet carpet cleaner. Wipe with the grain of the fabric. If you wipe against it, the fabric tears easily. Soak any remaining stain and press with a disposable diaper.

❻ Air the mattresses outside to remove any remaining smell.

❼ Clean your bathtub drain with Drano. The fecal matter can catch a hair clog and smell.

❽ Place towels over your child's bed if he has an upset stomach, especially over their upper legs and groin area. Often they will sit up and get sick in that exact spot.

❾ Place towels on the floor around a sick child's bed.

❿ Put a pull up on your sick child even if he is toilet trained. The diarrhea may catch him by surprise.

⑪ Get wrought iron lamps. They are difficult to break or dismantle and they still look attractive.

⑫ Get overhead lights. Consider recessed lights if your child hangs from the light.

The Child with Autism at Home

⓭ Watch the plumber the first time you have something stuck in the toilet. Have them teach you how to use an auger. Buy one.

⓮ Fix a dryer door that has been bent by the weight of your child by checking just above the hinges. There will be a bulge there from where the interior part of the hinge pushed against the door. Take a hammer and flatten to even with the rest of the dryer. Duct tape the door shut.

⓯ Salt raw eggs that fall on the floor. It breaks up the connectivity and allows you to clean it up more quickly.

⓰ Attach bookcases and curio cabinets to the wall. Your child could tip it over onto himself or others if he climbs up the shelving.

⓱ Tie the handles of a curio cabinet together with a ribbon tied in a square knot that will only get tighter if pulled upon.

⓲ Put away anything that you do not want to see broken.

⓳ Assign easy chores for your child to do. The following tips are chore suggestions for your child.

⓴ Place the pillow on his bed after you have made it.

50

⑪ The Broom Closet

㉑ Pull up the comforter after you've straightened the sheets.

㉒ Smooth out the wrinkles on the bed after you've pulled up the sheets.

㉓ Pull up the sheets and blankets.

㉔ Strip the sheets when they need to be washed.

㉕ Carry their dirty clothes to the hamper after they have changed into their pajamas.

㉖ Sort the laundry by color.

㉗ Drop the tablet or your pre-measured laundry detergent in the washing machine.

㉘ When they are old enough to reach into the washer, have them place the wet clothes in the dryer.

㉙ Add the dryer sheets.

㉚ Pick up toys and put them in the toy box.

㉛ Pick up trash and put it in the trash can.

㉜ Empty small trash baskets into a trash bag.

㉝ Hand you the dirty dishes.

The Child with Autism at Home

❸❹ Place dirty dishes in the dishwasher.

❸❺ Wash or dry the dishes.

❸❻ Hand you the clean dishes to put away.

12

The Front Door

Good manners are essential for a child with autism. It gives them a script of what is appropriate to say in social situations. Interactions with others are stressful. If children are polite, people love it and give them tremendous positive feedback. Their social confidence and acceptance rise.

❶ Be unfailingly polite when interacting with your child. They learn language in word groups. They will learn, "May I have some... please?" if you say it that way. They might not know what each word means, but they know this is how you ask for something you want.

❷ Say, "Thank you" whenever they hand you something, or do something you asked them to do.

❸ Say, "Great job," or "That's awesome," whenever you look at a project they are working on.

The Child with Autism at Home

❹ Say, "Are you alright?" every time they fall down or cry. Seeing another child hurt or crying can be very stressful. Some start crying or worse laughing when another child is crying. Learning the appropriate thing to say gives them a way of dealing with the situation and teaches them to show concern for others.

❺ Make comic or picture strips to illustrate when you would use common phrases.

❻ Teach them to look at you by saying, "Look at me." Place an M&M between your eyes. They get the M&M when they look at you.

❼ Make a game out of LOOK AT ME, and LOOK AWAY.

❽ Smile when they look at you. Put as much love as you can into your eyes.

❾ See if they are turning their ear to you slightly when they look away from you. Sometimes children with autism, if they want to understand what you are saying, look away at nothing to cut down on the input to the brain. They can concentrate better if all they are doing is listening.

❿ Do not make them look at you when you are angry.

❶ Teach them to say, "I'm sorry" when you are angry. Change your mood immediately upon hearing it. It is so vital to teach our children how to handle angry people that they meet in the world. Their lack of social skills may accidentally offend a classmate or someone in authority.

❷ Say, "Bless you!" when they sneeze. Have them say, "Bless you!" when you sneeze.

❸ Greet them with, "Good morning, (their name)" or, "Hello, (their name)." Teachers will train them to do that in school. Hearing it at home gives them a head start.

❹ Wave when you say, "Goodbye." Help them to wave back. It will help them deal with separation if they have something to do.

The Back Door

Some children with autism are born escape artists. This is particularly dangerous, because they have little sense of danger. The following is a list of tips on how to deal with such a child. Some of these tips may be against the fire code for your area. Please check. All these tips do is buy you time. Time to get to him before he leaves, and time to mature until he can recognize danger.

❶ Put a chain lock near the top of your doors.

❷ Place a door chime or bell that sounds when the door is opened.

❸ Put a buzzer alarm mat in the doorway.

❹ Put a wooden fence around your yard. Plastic ones are more easily broken, and chain link fences are full of footholds for small feet.

❺ Put chicken wire around the inside of the fence to eliminate any potential footholds.

❻ Staple the chicken wire to the fence.

❼ Use tent pegs to secure the base of the chicken wire.

❽ Keep recent photos available to show the police in case they get lost.

❾ Take regular walks with your child around your neighborhood. Hopefully he will come to get you when he wants to leave.

❿ Introduce your child to any neighbors that you meet on your walk. Describe the house that you live in. People forget numbers but remember descriptions.

⓫ Walk the same route every time. If he does leave the house alone, he will probably follow that route.

⓬ Pay attention to what interests him. Check those places first.

⓭ Check up in the trees, especially evergreen trees. They have numerous low branches for easy climbing.

⓮ Place a dog tag with his name, autism, and your cell phone number in the laces of his shoes.

The Child with Autism at Home

⓯ Pray. Remember even Mary and Joseph lost Jesus for three days. It can happen to anyone.

14

Resources

Children's Books & Other Materials

Children's books, teaching tools, and information about autism can be found in the following catalogs and websites:

❶ "Abilitations"- Call 1-800-850-8602 or visit www.abilitations.com.

❷ Autism-Aspergers Publishing Co. - Call 1-913-897-1004 or visit www.asperger.net.

❸ "Beyond Play" -Call 1-877-428-1244 or visit www.beyondplay.com.

❹ "Different Roads to Learning" -Call 1-800-853-1057 or visit www.difflearn.com.

❺ Future Horizons, Inc. -Call 1-800-489-0727 or visit www.FutureHorizons-autism.com.

❻ Jessica Kingsley Publications —Call 011-442-078332301 or visit www.jkp.com.

The Child with Autism at Home

❼ Labosh Publishing – Call 1-717-898-3813 or visit www.laboshpublishing.com.

❽ Mayer-Johnson Co. –Call 1-800-588-4548 or visit www.mayer-johnson.com.

❾ Phat Art 4 – Call 1-866-250-9878 or visit www.phatart4.com.

❿ "Pocket Full of Therapy" – Call 1-732-462-5888 or visit www.pfot.com.

⓫ "Special Needs Project" – Call 1-800-333-6867 or visit www.specialneeds.com.

⓬ Super Duper Publications – Call 1-800-277-8737 or visit www.superduperinc.com.

⓭ The Center for Speech and Language Disorders – Call 1-630-530-8551 or visit www.csld.com.

⓮ Woodbine House –Call 1-800-843-7323 or visit www.woodbinehouse.com.

Autism Resources

The ARC of the United States – Call 1-301-565-3842 or visit www.thearc.org.

Autism Research Institute – Fax 1-619-563-6840 or visit www.autism.com.

⑯ Resources

Autism Society of America – Call 1-800-3AUTISM or visit www.autism-society.org.

Bubel/Aiken Foundation – Call 1-224-430-0950 or visit www.thebubelaikenfoundation.org/home.htm

Doug Flutie Jr. Foundation – Call 1-866-3AUTISM orVisit www.dougflutiejrfoundation.org.

Unlocking Autism –Call 1-866-366-3361 or visit www.unlockingautism.org/main.asp.

LABOSH
B O O K L E T S

Look for additional Labosh Booklets in
The Child with Autism Series

The Child with Autism Goes on Vacation
The Go Everywhere Guide
Tips for Travel

The Child with Autism Goes to Town
The Go Anywhere Guide
250 Tips for Community Outings

The Child with Autism Learns the Faith
The Sunday School Guide
Tips and Lesson Plans

The Child with Autism Goes to Florida
The Theme Park Guide
Tips and Ride Reviews

Published by Labosh Publishing
PO Box 588,
East Petersburg, PA 17520-0588
www.laboshpublishing.com
email: info@laboshpublishing.com